THE
GREENISH-
OF S

THE LITTLE
GREENISH-BROWN
BOOK OF SLUGS

Compiled, Annotated

& Illustrated by

EVE CORBEL

SERIES EDITOR
STEPHEN OSBORNE
A LITTLE RED BOOK
ARSENAL PULP PRESS

A Little Red Book

THE LITTLE GREENISH-BROWN
BOOK OF SLUGS
TEXT AND ILLUSTRATIONS
COPYRIGHT © 1993
BY EVE CORBEL
All rights reserved.
ISBN 0-88978-267-9
CIP DATA: *see page 6*

LITTLE RED BOOKS
are published by
ARSENAL PULP PRESS
1062 HOMER STREET #100
VANCOUVER BC V6B 2W9
COVER DESIGN: *Kelly Brooks*
TYPESETTING: *Vancouver Desktop*
PRINTING: *Webcom*
PRINTED AND BOUND IN CANADA

TABLE OF CONTENTS

CANADIAN CATALOGUING
IN PUBLICATION DATA

Main entry under title:
The Little greenish-brown book of slugs
  (A Little red book)
  ISBN 0-88978-267-9
  1. Slugs (Mollusks)—Quotations, max-
ims, etc. 2. Slugs (Mollusks)—Humour.
3. Quotations, English. I. Corbel, Eve.
II. Series.
SB998.859L58 1993   632'.643
C93-091390-6

Fate is the Gardener

Not too long ago, the highest echelons of planetary life were presumed to be occupied by supernatural beings; in this enlightened age, of course, those echelons are the preserve of hockey players, movie stars, certain rock musicians and Paul Anka. The lower echelons on the other hand seem to have been occupied pretty well continuously by the crawling

and from time to time by insects like the flea or the gnat.

In an attempt to ascertain which of these lowly beasts might be counted as the lowliest, we turn to the great body of English Poetry, wherein we discover the flea to have at least one entire poem addressed to it, the gnat and the worm to have been honoured in countless metaphors (not the least of several written by Shakespeare himself) and the snake to have been immortalized in *Paradise Lost*, the best known and least read epic poem in the language. Of the slug, however, we find only a single dreary mention, in Samuel Taylor Coleridge, who wrote: "All nature seems at work. Slugs leave their lair"—in his perhaps aptly titled *Work Without Hope* of 1825.

With the help of the poetical record, then, let us claim for the slug the lowest of the echelons of hierarchy; which is as much as to say: the anchor, the foundation, of the great chain of echelons in which we are pleased to find ourselves only a step or two away from the top. In these pages you are invited—at your own leisure—to consider the lowly gastropod in all the complexity of its natural and imagined life—so that you might find new ways of considering the same complexities in the lives of those you love and those you are told to admire.

Represented in this volume are the

minds and works of more than a hundred thinkers who, over a period of more than a hundred years, have found in the slug an object worthy of contemplation, meditation and in some cases, strenuous action. Some of these notables have found themselves uplifted by the experience, while others have been humbled by it. Be assured: no one remains unaffected by such an exercise.

To some extent, of course, the history of our relationship with the slug might be said to be the history of our attempt to induce within the various species of slug the evolution of the much sought after Lettuce-Avoiding Gene, the Holy Grail of gardening peoples everywhere (see B. Carson,

Geist 1-4 for full literary exposition of this thesis). And, to the same extent, it remains the story of ambition, hubris and tragic defeat that continues to inform our sense of history, nature and the conflict that sets them against each other.

—*S. Osborne*

THE QUOTATIONS

WHAT WE KNOW OF SLUGS DOWN THROUGH THE AGES

There is no ancient lore concerning slugs.
—*Vancouver Magazine*

WHY THIS MIGHT BE SO

Let us accept slugs for what they are—slimy, ugly, voracious creatures. Not unlike people we owe money. —*Seattle P-I*

ON THE WONDROUS WORKINGS OF EVOLUTION

Slugs appear to have developed from snails, finding life easier by not having to carry their housing around with them.
—*Living Garden*

ON OUR GREATER HISTORICAL KNOWLEDGE OF THE LOWLY EARTHWORM

Volumes have been written about earthworms, but slugs? Forget it. —*Vancouver*

EFFECT ON SOCIAL STANDING

One simply does not champion the rights of slugs and expect to be invited to the best parties. —*Seattle P-I*

ON THE IMPLICATIONS OF THIS STATE OF AFFAIRS

Just last year a spokesperson for the United Nations told me slugs are not protected by international treaty.

—*Seattle P-I*

OR, TO GET MORE SPECIFIC

The pathetic, persecuted slug inspires only disgust and dies a murderous death without dignity. —*Vancouver Sun*

ON HOLDING VALUE OVER TIME

Slugs do not generally attract avid collectors. —*Oxford Book of Invertebrates*

HARD BODY PARTS ESSENTIAL TO THE FOSSIL RECORD

Uncertainty clouds the land slug's evolution. Lacking hard body parts, the slug has left no fossil record of its evolutionary path. —*Living Things*

WHAT THOSE SOFT BODY PARTS ACTUALLY DO

That slugs appear to creep on their belly surface is recognized in the name of the Class Gastropoda, from the Greek *gaster*, belly, and *pous, podos*, foot. The gastropod combines a skidding action of the rim of the foot along a sheet of mucus secreted at the anterior end with movement of muscular waves along the foot.

—*Simple Animals*

TRY THAT IN WORDS OF FEWER SYLLABLES?

The word gastropod means "belly foot" and refers to the way slugs, like Napoleon's army, walk on their stomachs.
—*Living Garden*

UNFORTUNATE SIDE EFFECT WITH MISTAKEN PHYLA

Often, slugs take the blame for other insects. —*Western Organic Gardening*

IS THAT ETYMOLOGY OR ENTOMOLOGY?

The word is akin to the Dutch *sluik* (lax, languid), to the Middle English *slugge* (sluggard), to the Swedish *slugga* (to be heavy and slow) and to the Old Germanic words for slow, dull and blunt. Hence the garden slug and, from the original shape, a bullet. —*Origins* (Partridge)

ON GETTING RIGHT IN THERE
FOR A CLOSE LOOK

There are a number of small creatures in the garden that crawl about as insects, feed as insects, and even resemble insects, but when you look closely, you realize they are *not* insects. —*Rodale's Guide*

ON NOT DRAWING TOO
FINE A DISTINCTION

But they can be considered honorary insects as far as their eating habits are concerned. —*Practical Gardener*

A UNIQUE CHARACTERISTIC

One of the few pests to bother the *Hosta undulata* is the slug. —*Plant Doctor*

MELODRAMATIC OVERTONES AT TIMES
ENTIRELY JUSTIFIED

Slugs are the desperate enemy of celery.
—*Cultivating Rough Ground*

WHEN IMPATIENCE CAN BE A VIRTUE

A slug will also eat a living animal if the creature will stay still long enough.

—*Curious Mollusks*

GARDENING TOO FREQUENTLY ACCOMPANIED BY HEARTBREAK

Slugs can wipe out an entire garden of seedlings in one night, as my heartbroken husband can testify. —*Garden Smarts*

VULNERABLE AT ALL THREE LEVELS

Some slugs ascend plants to feed on the leaves, often high above ground-level, others feed at or just below soil level, while the subterranean species attack roots and tubers often far beneath the surface of the ground.

—*Dictionary of Gardening*

JUST WHEN YOU THINK YOU CAN
HEAR A PIN DROP

You can hear them rasping away at plants.
—*Animal World*

BIG THOUGHTS ON THE ICKY SIDE

The true Pacific Northwest slug is just about the most repulsive looking critter

---

A RECORD OF UNRELENTING
RAVISHMENT

Boy, what they can do to lettuce!
—*Astrological Gardening*

Slugs gorge themselves on the foliage of young marigolds.   —*Plant Doctor*

75 percent of the first picking of strawberries was damaged by *Arion ater* and a few other slug species.   —*Harrowsmith*

---

on the planet. It is big and it is yellow and it is called the banana slug and it is really icky—but it is ours. —*Seattle P-I*

BIG THOUGHTS ON THE AWESOME SIDE

The degree of sophistication and complexity of their biological machinery is awe-inspiring. —*Vancouver Province*

Slugs pose a real danger to fledglings. Their slime gums up the young birds' feathers, and many either suffocate or starve. —*Vancouver Magazine*

In England and Wales slugs are responsible for the loss of 41,000 acre equivalents of wheat. —*Terrestrial Slugs*

Slugs have been recorded as causing widespread loss of brussels sprouts, cabbage, lettuce, bulbs and flowers. —*Terrestrial Slugs*

ALL BOIL DOWN TO PRETTY MUCH THE SAME THING

The whole body surface produces mucus.
— *Terrestrial Slugs*

SEARCH FOR THE PERFECT METAPHOR CONTINUES

A couple of researchers commented that the slug behaves as a well-nigh perfect wet-bulb thermometer. — *Harrowsmith*

SLUGS NON-SLUGS

Slugs are not a natural group of closely related animals; the term slug refers only to a body type.
— *Terrestrial Slugs*

AT TIMES YOU MAY BE TEMPTED TO ABANDON ALL HOPE

Deroceras reticulatum comes out at night and devours everything that grows.

Limax maximus is reported to have eaten worms, meat, snails, other slugs, all kinds of food scraps and even the bindings from old books.

—*Animal Kingdom*

MORE EFFICIENT THAN A SELF-CLEANING STOVE

When debris adheres to the slug's body it is capable of cleaning itself by moving the dirt backwards in the slime until a large hunk of debris-laden slime is at the tail.

—*Banana Slug*

PERHAPS THE BASIS
OF MORE THEORIES

Slugs do not feed when the relative humidity of the microhabitat is below 100%.
— *Terrestrial Slugs*

SOMETHING TO REMEMBER WHILE
YOU'RE TRYING TO GET CONTROL OF
THAT MICROHABITAT

A slug can devour a whole plant at one sitting. —*Rodale's Guide*

THE OPTIMISTIC
APPROACH

Slugs are choosy. They have strong food likes and dislikes. —*New York Times*

CONTRADICTED BY
THE EVIDENCE

One captive specimen of *Arion ater* consumed, with apparently equal relish, five other slugs, a dead mussel, insects, a scrap

of soap, dead mice, birds, earthworms, bread, wild plants, poisonous mushrooms, fern leaves, sea holly, a piece of newspaper and a handful of beach sand.
—*Animal Kingdom*

AND NOT
ONLY THAT

Meat and fish bones left lying about by the dog or cat, plum stones left after jam making, vegetable and fruit peelings, curdled milk and dog biscuits. —*New Biology VI*

Oxychilus cellarius is quite capable of killing and eating butterflies. —*Animal Kingdom*

ANY ENEMY OF THEIRS, ETC.

Slugs are eaten by a variety of predators, including frogs, toads, hedgehogs, ducks, blackbirds, thrushes and other birds.
                                    —*International Wildlife*

Some slugs are eaten by badgers, shrews, moles and mice.
                                    —*Discovering Slugs*

Firefly larvae feed upon and kill them.
                                    —*Curious Mollusks*

They are also attacked by centipedes, certain beetles and carnivorous slugs and snails.   —*Discovering Slugs*

WHAT WE KNOW WITHOUT HAVING TO
RESORT TO THE SCIENTIFIC METHOD
Slugs are not easy to eat.
                                    —*Discovering Slugs*

Predaceous insects, such as carabid and staphylinid beetle larvae, have been observed feeding on live slugs.

—*Terrestrial Slugs*

If the garden area is fenced to keep out dogs, turtles are quite beneficial and seldom seen.

—*Vegetable Growing Handbook*

Porcupines help reduce their numbers.

—*Organic Garden Book*

Domestic ducks will scoop up slugs by the dozen.

—*Living Things*

HOW LESSER ORDERS FIND OUT

Dogs and ducks have been seen gagging when they tried to eat a banana slug.

—*Banana Slug*

LITTLE KNOWN DISGUSTING FACTS

Some slugs eat their own slime, at least when in captivity—sometimes a slug will begin to eat slime from another slug, then devour its skin, and finally feast on the remains. —*Curious Mollusks*

CERTAIN CROPS MORE LIKELY TO BE IMMUNE?

They avoid plants with stinging hairs such as the stinging nettle, borage and older cucumber plants.

—*Companion Planting*

UNCERTAINTY PRINCIPLE STILL AT WORK IN NATURE

Slugs that had been feeding mainly on stinging nettle in the wild sometimes preferred buttercup leaves in the laboratory, and vice versa. —*Terrestrial Slugs*

Slugs can be said to cause a loss of about 36,000 tons of potatoes each year—the average annual consumption of about 400,000 people.

—*Terrestrial Slugs*

NECESSITY ALWAYS THE MOTHER OF SOMETHING OR OTHER

The indigenous Yuroks of the North Coast area would use the banana slug for food when other food became scarce.

—*Banana Slug*

THE LOVE LIFE OF A SLUG:
SOME SALACIOUS DETAILS

In some species of *Arion* there is an ever-tile sarcobelum on the wall of the penis sac; and in *Vaginulus* there is a dart sac with a calcified dart.

In *Arion ater* the first sign of courtship is one animal pursuing another, often eating the mucus trail.

The courting ritual may include lunging, biting, mantle-flapping, and tail-wagging.

—Terrestrial Slugs

Some premating biting becomes quite violent: actual hunks of flesh can be bitten off, leaving each slug battered and scarred. *—Banana Slug*

SOME NATURAL ENEMIES OF SLUGS

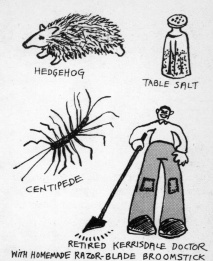

HEDGEHOG

TABLE SALT

CENTIPEDE

RETIRED KERRISDALE DOCTOR
WITH HOMEMADE RAZOR-BLADE BROOMSTICK

AND THEN YOU JUST
CLOSE YOUR EYES
AND GULP

German immigrant families in the 1800s and early 1900s ate banana slugs by removing the slime with vinegar, gutting them like fish and deep-frying them in a batter. —*Banana Slug*

PROOF THAT
CALIFORNIA CELEBRITIES
HAVE TOO MUCH TIME
ON THEIR HANDS

One northern California slug festival features a slug recipe contest with celebrities acting as tasters and judges. Banana slugs are gathered in the woods, confined a few days, killed and cooked.

—*Banana Slug*

They wrap their bodies together in a mass of slime.   *—Discovering Slugs*

They extend their sex organs by turning them inside out, as one turns out a glove finger.   *—International Wildlife*

The fully extended sex organs assume an irregular shape and become pearly white with iridescent shades of pink, blue and green.   *—International Wildlife*

They exchange sperm masses.
    —International Wildlife

Ariolimax often attempt and achieve appophalation: that is, one manages to gnaw off the penis of the other.
    —Animal World

LOTUS LAND NOT FOR THE
SQUEAMISHLY-MINDED

Coastal B.C. supports the largest number of slugs in Canada—as many as three per square foot of garden soil. —*Harrowsmith*

ONE LAST REFUGE FOR THE
SQUEAMISHLY-MINDED

Only the Prairie provinces with their hot, dry summers and bitterly cold winters are wholly unpopular with slugs.

—*Harrowsmith*

ANOTHER WAY TO
GIVE ONESELF
THE CREEPS

The eyes, on the end of long tentacles, look rather like little black pin heads. If you touch one gently, sometimes one eye will be pulled back while the other watches you. —*Snails and Slugs*

After a short time the love-play passes into a love-duel; each slug projects its calcareous love-dart into the sole of the partner. —*The Young Specialist*

As the embrace is complete, the bag of living water is drawn up and re-absorbed. The process is lengthy, lovely and moving, almost lyrical.

—*Vancouver Sun*

After a 1/2–2 1/2-hour courtship, a pair of slugs dangle on a cord of slime, their bodies constantly writhing at a pace that puts their usual slow movements to shame.

—*International Wildlife*

ON WHAT A LITTLE PRACTICE
CAN DO FOR ONE

The different species in these three families can be distinguished after a little practice by their general colour, the colour of the foot, the texture of the skin and the colour of the slime they produce.
—*New Biology VI*

ON THE NET EFFECT OF PREDATORS ON
SLUG DEMOGRAPHICS

No natural enemy of slugs is effective in keeping their numbers in check.
—*Dictionary of Gardening*

ON WHERE THE NUMBERS COME FROM

The mating season of the Grey Field Slug is "when the gorse is out in flower"—that is, mating takes place during every month of the year. —*New Biology*

INTERESTING THINGS YOU CAN
DO WITH SLUGS

Keep them in almost any large wooden box or old fish tank. Even an old plastic sandwich box will do. —*Snails and Slugs*

Allow the animal to extend fully on the end of a stick and then plunge the stick into boiling water.

—*Invertebrate Anatomy*

The blood vessels can be readily studied by injecting them with liquids such as Indian ink or, if a permanent specimen is required, rubber latex.

—*Terrestrial Slugs*

The grey field slug can be gathered up, unseen, and be frozen or canned along with the food. —*Curious Mollusks*

SOME LITTLE-KNOWN
FACTS OF INTEREST

If one of the optic tentacles is removed and the slugs are illuminated from above they crawl round in circles, always crawling to the eyeless side.

A slug's heart is myogenic; i.e. it will continue beating when removed from the body.

Slugs can withstand total immersion in water at 10°C for over five hours.

—*Terrestrial Slugs*

AND THE ROLE OF GENDER EQUALITY

Slugs have both sexes in the same animal. Even so, each seeks out another individual to mate with. —*Animal World*

ON THE POSSIBILITY OF EVER GETTING THEM DOWN TO JUST ONE LAST SLUG

They can even fertilize *themselves* in adverse conditions. —*International Wildlife*

HOW GENDER EQUALITY WORKS, SORT OF

The youngest slugs are male, the oldest are female, and those in between have the capabilities of both sexes. All this means that they reproduce very efficiently.
—*Controlling Vegetable Pests*

QUESTIONS ARISING FROM THEIR HERMAPHRODITIC NATURE

Both partners are fertilized during copulation, giving rise to the question: who did what to whom with what?
—*Vancouver Magazine*

SOME GRAND
ANCESTRAL REMEDIES

For many centuries slugs were regarded as a sovereign remedy for a variety of ailments, eaten alive or boiled in milk for the cure of tuberculosis, for example.

They were once eaten in the form of ashes to relieve such diverse ills as ulcers, dysentery or hydrocephalus.

As Pliny recorded, quick relief could be obtained if the little chalky grains representing the slug's internal shell were placed in a hollow tooth.

One cure for warts in recent use involved rubbing the wart with a slug and then impaling the slug on a thorn. As it died and withered away, so did the wart.

—*International Wildlife*

On wet autumn mornings many circular patches of mucus may be visible, indicating extensive nocturnal courting.

—*Terrestrial Slugs*

Not quite throwing in the towel: Grow plants that are not attractive to slugs or not harmed by their presence. Omit flowers and vegetables.

—*Vancouver Province*

DISCOURAGEMENT
BY VEGETATION

Tansy, a pretty herb, discourages slugs.
—*Easy Gardening*

Slugs love to hide under geraniums and ivy. If you haven't planted them, don't.
—*Garden Smarts*

Slugs dislike certain aromatic plants: the common sage is particularly effective, as is the scarlet sage. Try also thyme and hyssop. —*Garden Wisdom*

Hellebore keeps slugs from grape vines.
—*Ecological Gardening*

ONE WAY OF DEALING WITH THE UNCERTAINTY PRINCIPLE

Dependent on crossed trails, slug mating is uncertain and infrequent, so the creatures double their chances in copulation by being hermaphroditic. —*Harrowsmith*

BUT LEST YE FORGET

Humans have courtship habits far stranger even than those of the slug.
—*Weekender's Gardening Manual*

Because they suffer from a "Dracula complex" (avoiding light), they seek out cool, moist, dark conditions. —*Q & A*

HARDER TO COUNT BEFORE THEY HATCH

Slug eggs, laid near the soil surface, look like a gelatinous mass of pearly white BBs.
—*Controlling Vegetable Pests*

WHERE TO FIND THEM, IF YOU'RE GOING TO GET SERIOUS ABOUT ALL THIS

They are laid in batches of 20 to 300 in damp, sheltered places, look like tiny translucent balls of jelly, and are far more resistant to heat, cold and drying than are the slugs that laid them. —*Harrowsmith*

Suddenly, it seems, slugs are chic.
—*Living Things*

WHAT TO EXPECT WHEN YOU FIND A SLUG IN YOUR DING DONGS

The slug was discovered when 14-year-old Robbie Kujala reached into a Hostess box Friday night to grab a snack and discovered a black slug already munching its way through the chocolate Ding Dongs.

"The slug was all curled up—it was the size of a ping pong ball," his mother, Carol, said.

"It was just sickening. Somebody has to do something about this. I'm very angry that something like this could happen."
—*Vancouver Sun*, May 1981

DESPERATE MEASURES
FOR DESPERATE TIMES

Seedlings or shoots can be surrounded with plastic bottles which have been cut off at the bottom. Spreading a mulch of ornamental pine bark is also effective.
—*Organic Garden Book*

Slugs actually get an electric shock when they touch copper. It's theorized that the slugs' slimy coating interacts chemically with the copper, creating an electric current.
—*Rodale's Chemical-Free Yard*

ON THE LIKELIHOOD THAT FINDING
THEM WILL HAVE ANY EFFECT

Even if you disposed of all but one *Agriolimax agrestis*, that one grey slug would still be capable of laying up to 100 eggs, and some eggs could even contain twins.
—*New York Times*

Push four- to eight-inch copper strips into soil as edging for garden beds.
—*Rodale's Chemical-Free Yard*

Powdered copper sulphate forms a barrier which the slugs will not cross.
—*Vancouver Sun*

Place Tree Tanglefoot on the stem of the plant to prevent slugs from crawling up to feast on tender growth.
—*Astrological Gardening*

PROJECT FOR A QUIET AFTERNOON

Open the animal by a longitudinal mid-dorsal incision from the top of the head to the tip of the tail, and pin aside the flaps. Notice the extensive perivisceral cavity (haemocoel) formed of the large blood lacunae. Trace the course of the alimentary canal. —*Invertebrate Anatomy*

MAXIMUM SPEEDS OF SOME ANIMALS

HOUSE CAT
30 mph

CHARGING
ELEPHANT
25 mph

CHICKEN
9 mph

3-TOED SLOTH
.15 mph

SLUG
0.03 mph

(N.B: Diagrams not to scale.)

PROSPECTS BLEAK FOR LIMAX FLAVUS

Since scientists have discovered important cancer-treating chemicals in our lovable *limax flavus*, it is inevitable that many thousands of slugs will be maltreated, mutilated and murdered in the name of research. —*Vancouver Sun*

A SPIN DOCTOR'S TAKE ON IT

The slug has to work hard on its chronic image problem. —*Vancouver Province*

ON THE VIRTUES OF HAVING AN ABUNDANT SUPPLY OF SLUG SLIME

Ingrith Deyrup-Olsen has been conducting experiments for three years on her abundant supply of slug slime, in hopes it may lead to a cure for cystic fibrosis.
—*Vancouver Province*

SOMEWHAT MORE STATELY THAN
THE SUBMARINE RACES

I find it relaxing to pull up a chair on the deck, in the glow of the outdoor floodlight, and watch the slugs come up and over a plank and down the other side, resurfacing on the next plank, and the next, moving very much like a school of dolphins rising and diving down below the waves. —*Vancouver Sun*

THE SMOKE AND MIRRORS APPROACH

To save my flowers, I plant cabbage in the same area. Most of the slugs attack the cabbage, not the flowers. —*Garden Smarts*

OR YOU MIGHT CONSIDER
GROWTH HORMONES

Grow flowers that slugs either do not like or cannot eat fast enough to deter growth: ageratum, alyssum, begonia, cosmos,

impatiens, opal basil and torenia.
—*New York Times*

SOMETHING TO REMEMBER OUT
ON THE TRAPLINE

Slugs tend to advance toward specific targets. —*Western Organic Gardening*

POSSIBLE APPLICATION FOR
ZENO'S PARADOX

A slug can lose up to one-fifth of its body weight in producing slime for a forty-minute crawl. —*New York Times*

THE HANDICAPPER'S LINE

Limax maximus, the speediest of slugs, can travel at a speed of only about 10 inches a minute, while its nearest rivals on this continent, the black slug and the banana slug, travel at the modest snail's pace of three and four inches a minute, respectively. —*Harrowsmith*

THE USUAL
BEERY NOSTRUMS

Put beer in saucers to attract slugs.
—*New Victory Garden*

The slug crawls in and drowns—but he goes under while telling old jokes and singing college fight songs.   —*Seattle P-I*

The next morning the beer should be filled with slugs, and vice versa.
—*Suzanne's Garden Secrets*

One has the feeling that at least there has been no unnecessary suffering.
—*London Observer*

If it appears that they are taking a sip and then leaving, mix in a bit of pastry flour to make a sticky mixture.
—*The Mulch Book*

WHEN THE FIX IS IN

While he's running, you must stroke his body just below his airhole. It makes him go faster. —slug owner Ron Massey, *Vancouver Province*

MORE TRAPLINE TIPS

Some slugs have been observed following slime trails to find their way back to shelter. —*Living Things*

CREATE YOUR OWN DMZ

Clear a strip one yard wide around your vegetable patch to help prevent entry of slugs from adjacent weedy or landscaped areas. Till the strip frequently.

—*Controlling Vegetable Pests*

WHY WE CALL THEM PESKY DEVILS

One year we interplanted bibb lettuce and Florence fennel, and we noticed that no slugs attacked the lettuce. We tried the combination again, and this time the slugs did attack the lettuce. —*Growing Food the Natural Way*

ON THE LACERATING EFFECTS OF GROUND-UP SKELETONS

Diatomaceous earth is made from the ground skeletons of small fossilized animals. When soft-bodied slugs come in contact with it, its sharp edges lacerate their exoskeletons. —*Rodale's Guide*

AND ONE UNPLEASANT SIDE EFFECT

Diatomaceous earth can cause serious, permanent damage to the lining of one's lungs if inhaled. —*Harrowsmith*

AND ANOTHER

And it is very expensive. —*Rodale's Guide*

IF ALL ELSE FAILS, OR
MAYBE JUST BEFORE THAT

Try three tablespoons of Epsom salts to one gallon of water. Pour it over those areas where you think the slugs are hiding out. —*Suzanne's Garden Secrets*

YOU CAN STILL REACH FOR THE
WORMWOOD

They avoid a soil drench of wormwood tea. —*The Mulch Book*

OR EVEN THE TOBACCO CAN

Strew some tobacco dust over all the branches and leaves; let this remain two or three days, then you may wash it off.
                    —*Every Man His Own Gardener*

OR ANYTHING ELSE THAT
COMES TO HAND

Sprinkle with ginger.   *—Vancouver Sun*

Oak leaves or wood shavings.
                    —Ecological Gardening

Rough bark, human hair, crushed egg-
shells.   *—Oriental Vegetables*

Bands of fibreglass tucked around plants.
                    —Harrowsmith

Zinc collars.   *—Huxley's Encyclopedia*

Lime or cinders, for slugs don't like to
have their tummies tickled.
                    —Chatelaine's Gardening

Create a "slug salad" from tender young lettuce, bean shoots and so on, and place it in a heap on the soil near to the plants. The next morning, the congregation of slugs can be removed. —*Garden Wisdom*

OFFICIAL RESPONSE TO
THE SLUG IN
THE DING DONGS

"We're looking at the store, the distributor and the manufacturer," said Ray Wong, Burnaby health inspector.

Wong said he doesn't think the slug got into the box while it was in the Kujala house. "Which makes it very mysterious as to how it got in there."

Said Jack Warn, sales manager of Francis

SOMETHING TO REMEMBER WHEN
FEELING SUICIDAL

Slugs will cross dust and powder barriers if they get hungry enough. —*Rodale's Chemical-Free Yard*

Distributors, "It's the first time I've ever seen anything like that and I've been in the business 20 years."

Tom Cantafio, manager of the Safeway store, where the package was purchased, said he has had no other complaints about Ding Dongs.

Rod Taylor, spokesman for the Seattle bakery, ITT Continental Baking Co., was reserving judgment until he found out more about the incident.

—*Vancouver Sun*

SO MUCH FOR THE
STALE BEER THEORY

Dainton records that she has never seen slugs drinking. —*Terrestrial Slugs*

THE IRRITATING THING ABOUT
IRRITANT THEORY

They can readily cast off irritants with the slime that they excrete. —*Dictionary of Gardening*

AND YES THERE IS SOMETHING MORE
TO THE SLIME THING

A slug moves upon its own band of slime, a "carpet" of its own making. So even if you let the animal creep over a razor blade, it will not take the slightest harm from the sharp edge.

—*The Young Specialist*

YOU CAN ALWAYS TRY THE INDIVIDUAL
HOUSING APPROACH

Surround the young plants with roofing slates or some similar thin flat material and cover them with a paste made up of thick oil and soot. —*Garden Wisdom*

Salt turns their bodies orange.
                                —*Wise Garden*

A night walk with the flashlight should reveal these guys. You can control them with a salt shaker.   —*Plant Doctor*

Salt causes slugs to produce great quantities of slime, and they destroy themselves through desiccation.
                        —*Gardening Know-How*

The slug immediately shrivels, curls up, and looks as if it is dead. *It is not.* Within an hour or two the slug manufactures another coat of slime and continues on his merry way.   —*Langley Advance*

Salting is hardly a one-shot cure, and I began to wonder what effect a nightly dusting of salt would have on my garden.
                                —*Harrowsmith*

YOU CAN TRY DECEPTION

Discourage slugs by watering early in the morning to allow soaking-in time before nightfall. —*How to Get Your Lawn & Garden Off Drugs*

AND DECEIT

Place boards between garden rows for the slugs to hide under during the heat of the day. Turn them over daily and dispatch the slugs.—*Vegetables*

OR SUBTERFUGE

Scatter cabbage or lettuce leaves at night and pick up the slugs underneath them in the morning. —*Backyard Vegetable Factory*

AND CAMOUFLAGE

A hollowed-out and inverted half-grapefruit rind can be used as an organic trap.
—*Living Things*

BUT IN THE END YOU MAY HAVE TO REMEMBER

Trapping does not catch many underground slugs, nor does it prevent invasion from elsewhere. —*Vancouver Sun*

TRY GOING TO THE SOURCE

Eliminate the eggs, which look like tiny, clear glass marbles and are usually found in groups of one hundred or more. If you find one or two, dig around the area to see if you can find more. Throw each and every one away. —*Weekender's Gardening Manual*

THE LABOUR-INTENSIVE REMEDY

Handpicking these slimy vegetarians is the safest way to protect the crop. —*New Victory Garden*

WITH CAVEAT

If you can bring yourself to touch them.

—Easy Gardening

A CERTAIN FINE RAGE

Get after them with your stomping slippers! *—Ecological Gardening*

Feed them to the chickens!
—Oriental Vegetables

Stab them with a hat-pin after dark!
—Dictionary of Gardening

Drive them out onto the road with a nine iron! *—Vancouver Magazine*

AN OPTIMISTIC NOTE

Slugs can be eliminated in three years by assiduous handpicking.
—*Ecological Gardening*

Pierce them with a sharpened stick with a twelve-inch needle-sharp spike on the end—slug shishkabob!
—*Ecological Gardening*

An old pair of needle-nosed pliers!
—*Harrowsmith*

Flush them down the toilet! Pitch them into the yard next door! Nail them with your Weed-Eater!
—*Vancouver Magazine*

SURE, TRY TELLING GEORGE THAT

In 1977 the grey field slug destroyed most of George Munroyd's garden vegetables in spite of the hand-picking undertaken.

—*Living Garden*

THE PURE
EXISTENTIAL TRUTH

One garden in Harpenden was sampled 41, 58, 53 and 46 times in successive years and the total number of slugs collected and removed varied between ten thousand and nearly seventeen thousand a year. In spite of removing average half-hour samples of 256, 293, 257 and 259, *no reduction in population was observable.*

—*New Biology VI*

CONSIDER THOSE MORE
DELICATE SENSIBILITIES

If the sight of a pan full of stale beer and dead slugs offends your delicate sensibilities, a jar made of opaque glass will do as well. Then when the time comes to remove it, you can slap on the lid without looking inside and toss it in the garbage can. (The waste of a recyclable jar will be on your conscience.) —*Growing Vegetables*

AND THEN THOSE
LESS DELICATE ONES

You try a beer trap here in the Pacific Northwest and you'll find it empty and one large slug demanding to know what kind of establishment runs out of beer so early. —*Vancouver Sun*

HOW TO GIVE ONESELF THE CREEPS
AFTER MIDNIGHT

Apparently, some slugs are teetotalers. Ken Johnston of West Salem, Wisconsin, had no luck with beer. In fact, he counted over a thousand slugs in the garden in just four nights. —*Garden Smarts*

CONTRADICTORY OUTCOMES OF
TIDINESS THEORY

Remove hiding places by keeping your garden free of debris, which slugs need for shade during the day.

—Chatelaine's Gardening

Never leave cabbage stalks, etc., lying about. *—ABC of Gardening*

Slugs in an untidy garden are frequently much less harmful than in a well-kept one, as they eat whatever lies in their way. *—New Biology VI*

If the garden beds are kept tidy, if grass cuttings and old leaves are cleared away, there is no natural food for the slugs and they turn to the tender parts of cultivated plants. *—Living Garden*

SCIENTIST IN NEED OF MEANINGFUL RESEARCH PROJECT

In one British scientist's experiment, slugs turned their antennae up at Guinness stout, cider and two English bitters. Gin and tonic and lagers were more popular, but Kaliber, an alcohol-free brew by Guinness, beat them all by claiming thirty-three victims. —*Vancouver Sun*

THEN THERE'S ALWAYS THE DIRECT APPROACH

Go to the shelf, buy some slug bait and read the directions. —*Harrowsmith*

WHILE REMEMBERING ALL THE WHILE

Slugs are immune to most pesticides.
—*Vancouver Province*

HOW TO SPEND A PLEASANT AFTERNOON

20 lbs. of bran should be damped with a gallon of water and 1 lb. of Paris green

stirred in. This mixture is sufficient dressing for one acre of garden.

—*ABC of Gardening*

LITTLE HEADWAY ON
THE MULCHING CONTROVERSY

Copious mulching keeps down weeds and slowly fertilizes the soil, but slugs congregate in slimy abundance under the mulch.
—*Harrowsmith*

I've mulched for many years and have no slugs in my garden. A well-mulched garden, after there is plenty of humus in the soil, attracts earthworms and that tends to make the soil alkaline, which slugs don't like. Isn't that a break?
—*The Ruth Stout No-Work Garden Book*

SPECIAL TOOLS FOR
SPECIAL TASKS

A few inches of kerosene in a bucket is an effective exterminator for all garden pests. If you do not like to handle the slugs then purchase a pair of food tongs which will do the job very nicely. —*Western Organic Gardening*

SURE, UNTIL
THE WIND SHIFTS

Slug-Off will mask the odour of the attracting plant and thus deter the attacking slugs. —*Wise Garden*

ON THE VIRTUE OF HAVING NO
SECOND THOUGHTS

After all the hard work of preparing the soil, digging, and planting, I'm not about to start all over again for lack of a little slug bait. —*Bill Vander Zalm*

WHAT TO EXPECT WHEN THE SLUG THAT WAS IN ONE'S DING DONGS DISAPPEARS

Some time after the box was taken to the health unit, health workers discovered the slug was missing.

"They called and told us they had lost the slug, so nothing can be done," said Kujala. "Isn't that maddening? Isn't that absurd? I should never have given the slug to them. They said they opened the box today and it wasn't in the box," she said.

LITTLE-KNOWN UNPLEASANT SIDE EFFECT

Never apply slug bait when dogs are present: it may look as though you're putting out dry dog food. —*Sunset New Western Garden*

"It's awful curious. We had it five days and it didn't move out of the box all that time."

With the loss of the slug the investigation is now stymied, Health Inspector Ray Wong said.

Robert Keane, vice-president of public affairs for ITT Continental Baking Co. at the company's head office in Rye, New York, said earlier that he was "trying to ascertain what the origin of the slug is."
—*Vancouver Sun*

MORE GRISLY DETAIL

The bait both paralyzes slugs and acts as a stomach poison. Paralyzed slugs then succumb to a combination of the effects of the poison and desiccation when exposed to sunlight. —*Harrowsmith*

LET THE EMPTOR
ALWAYS CAVEAT

If the dosage is too light and the next day overcast and moist, however, many slugs recover. —*Harrowsmith*

NOT TO MENTION
THE POOR PREDATOR

Dying slugs which have been poisoned by slug bait are a hazard to creatures which eat slugs. —*Companion Planting*

A FINE
TACTICAL POINT

If you give a slug a choice between lush, succulent growth of a plant that it likes, on the one hand, and a heap of slug bait on the other, it will go to the growing plant in the majority of cases.

—*Vancouver Province*

The bait kills slugs in the garden, but draws more from the surrounding countryside. Once baiting is started, it has to be continued in order to keep the garden safe. —*Living Garden*

The average slug is a vegetarian pacifist.
—*Seattle P-I*

THE PINE-SOL
METAPHOR

Continued use of the metaldehyde method is rather like continually pouring a disinfectant down a drain whenever it offends without ever trying to understand, and then prevent, the cause of the smell.

—*New Biology VI*

REVERT TO ANCIENT
SEIGE WARFARE

Dig a trench around your garden and line it with plastic. The trench will fill with water and drown the slugs.

—*Vancouver Province*

DOUBLE TROUBLE BOIL
AND BUBBLE, OR
WHATEVER IT WAS

Tip them into a pail of boiling water. Pour the brew over compost to enrich it, or leave the pail standing for a few days until

its contents start to smell strongly, then pour the brew around endangered crops at a suitable interval before harvesting. The liquid will ward off slugs, even when thinly spread. —*Companion Planting*

RED IN TOOTH
AND CLAW:
OR BACK TO BASICS

Maybe I was up earlier than usual. Maybe I was peering under a leaf. But there it was, slimy, oozing a sticky trail from its yucky soft body. Without hesitating, I picked it up and stepped on it. I was blooded, as they say in hunting.

—*Ecological Gardening*

GRAND ANCESTRAL TECHNIQUE
ALWAYS A GOOD BET

The mechanical action of implements and trampling cows must kill a number of slugs. —*Terrestrial Slugs*

THEN THERE'S THE HI-TECH
APPROACH TECHNIQUE

The electric fence technique keeps slugs away: a two-inch-high barrier incorporating two metal strips is powered by a small battery. —*Huxley's Encyclopedia*

Some slugs can be goaded into attacking, and to humans the bite feels like a sharp needle drawn over the skin. —*Vancouver Magazine*

LET YOUR IMAGINATION RUN WILD

Organic gardeners have come up with weird concoctions for sprays. These in-

clude mixing hot pepper sauce, garlic, and even ground slugs—a rather offensive lot to put in your blender; this approach, however, does have the virtues of being safe and inexpensive.
—*Weekender's Gardening Manual*

IF THERE IS A FABLE TO BE FOUND IN ANY OF THIS

All these remedies depend on one thing: the strength of the stomach of the gardener. —*London Observer*

WHEN ALL ELSE FAILS, TRY BECOMING THE PROBLEM

There was a time when we thought we had a slug problem, they annoyed us so. However, we brought the problem under control more by changing our attitude than by controlling the slugs. —*Gardening for Independence*

OR IF YOU CAN'T ALTER YOUR MIND
YOU MIGHT TRY ROCK GARDENING

For the most part slugs are more unsightly than damaging.

—*Western Organic Gardening*

PROOF AGAIN THAT
MIGHT MAKES RIGHT

One little ear shell slug, taken from its home in the dirt by a biologist, frothed at the mouth and spat out from its stomach what was left of its last meal. Being a bit larger, the biologist won the fight.

—*Curious Mollusks*

ISN'T BEING BITTEN AND
SPAT UPON ENOUGH?

There is no record of any citizen having been killed, assaulted or even slapped around by a slug. The hatred is ours.

—*Seattle P-I*

ESPECIALLY TO ANOTHER INVERTEBRATE

The sleek contours of their bodies and the special adaptations they show to their particular way of life surely should command something other than a shudder.

—*Oxford Book of Invertebrates*

SCIENTISTS GROWING INCREASINGLY DESPERATE FOR INSTRUCTION

AT&T's Bell Laboratories scientists are hoping slugs might teach them how to develop artificial intelligence in computers. —*Vancouver Sun*

THEN THERE'S THE LARGER RHETORICAL VIEW

Who has ever been slimed to death by a herd of slugs, or when has a slug the size of a bus attacked Tokyo?

—*Vancouver Magazine*

NOT TO MENTION THE FUTURE OF THE
REDWOOD FOREST

Banana slugs deposit a valuable nitrogen-rich fertilizer in their droppings, giving young redwood trees a boost in growth.

—*Banana Slug*

PRAY FOR THE
HAPLESS ENTREPRENEUR

Arion ater became so abundant in Abbotsford at one time that a motel owner was forced out of business.

—*Vancouver Magazine*

ANY GOOD SLUG BOOK HAS TO HAVE THE
WORD *UNDULATE* IN IT SOMEWHERE

We once saw a slug crawl, with no hesitation, into a puddle and swim (undulating like a seal) through about 20 inches of deep water. —*Banana Slug*

THE WORLD DISCOVERED TO BE LESS
SECURE PERHAPS THAN WE MIGHT HAVE
BEEN LED TO BELIEVE

Members of the family Vitrinidae range
into the Arctic and can sometimes be seen
gliding along on the surface of snow.

ONE OR TWO THINGS,
AT LEAST,
REMAIN ETERNAL

There are pro-slug and anti-slug forces
growing, said Wendy Morton.

—*Vancouver Province*

WHAT YOU OUGHT TO CALL THEM:
A FEW KNOWN VARIETIES OF
THE WORLD'S SLUGS

Scientific Name	Common Name
Anadenulus cockerelli	American keeled slug
Arion ater	black arion
Arion circumscriptus	brown-banded arion
Arion distinctus	darkface arion
Arion fasciatus	orange-banded arion
Arion hortensis	garden arion
Arion intermedius	hedgehog arion
Arion owenii	warty arion
Arion rufus	chocolate arion
Arion subfuscus	dusky arion
Arion sylvaticus	forest arion
Ariolimax californicus	California banana slug
Ariolimax columbianus	Pacific banana slug
Ariolimax dolichophallus	slender banana slug
Binneya guadalupensis	Guadalupe shelled slug
Binneya notabilis	Santa Barbara shelled slug
Hemphillia burringtoni	keeled jumping-slug
Hemphillia camelus	pale jumping-slug
Hemphillia danielsi	marbled jumping-slug
Hemphillia dromedarius	dromedary jumping-slug

Hemphillia glandulosa	warty jumping-slug
Hemphillia malonei	Malone jumping-slug
Hemphillia pantherina	panther jumping-slug
Hesperarion hemphilli	Hemphill slug
Hesperarion niger	black slug
Magnipelta mycophaga	spotted slug
Prophysaon andersoni	reticulate taildropper
Prophysaon boreale	northern taildropper
Prophysaon coeruleum	blue-grey taildropper
Prophysaon dubium	papillose taildropper
Prophysaon fasciatum	banded taildropper
Prophysaon foliolatum	yellow-bordered taildropper
Prophysaon humile	smoky taildropper
Prophysaon obscurum	mottled taildropper
Prophysaon vanattae	scarletback taildropper
Megapallifera mutabilis	changeable mantle slug
Megapallifera ragsdalei	Ozark mantle slug
Megapallifera wetherbyi	blotchy mantle slug
Pallifera dorsalis	pale mantle slug
Pallifera fosteri	Foster mantle slug
Pallifera hemphilli	black mantle slug
Pallifera marmorea	marbled mantle slug
Pallifera ohioensis	redfoot mantle slug
Pallifera pilsbryi	Arizona mantle slug

Pallifera secreta	severed mantle slug
Pallifera varia	variable mantle slug
Philomycus carolinianus	Carolina mantle slug
Philomycus flexuolaris	winding mantle slug
Philomycus sellatus	Alabama mantle slug
Philomycus togatus	toga mantle slug
Philomycus venustus	brown-spotted mantle slug
Philomycus virginicus	Virginia mantle slug
Zacoleus idahoensis	sheathed slug

—from *Mollusks*

SOURCES

A to Z Hints for the Vegetable Gardener. Robert E. Sanders. Des Moines IA: Garden Way, 1976

ABC of Gardening. W. E. Shewell-Cooper. London: English Universities Press Ltd., 1946

Astrological Gardening. Louise Riotte. Pownal VT: Storey Communications, 1989

Backyard Vegetable Factory. Duane Newcomb. Emmaus PA: Rodale, 1988

Chatelaine's Gardening Book. Lois Wilson. Toronto: Maclean-Hunter, 1970

City Gardener's Handbook. Linda Yang. New York: Random House, 1990

City People's Book of Raising Food. Helga and William Olkowski. Emmaus PA: Rodale, 1975

Companion Planting: Successful Gardening the Organic Way. Gertrud Franck. NY: Thorsons, 1983

Complete Vegetable Gardener's Sourcebook. Duane Newcomb. New York: Avon, 1980

Controlling Vegetable Pests. Cynthia Putnam, ed. San Ramon CA: Ortho Books, 1991

Cultivating Rough Ground. Keith Wills. Wellingborough, Northamptonshire: Thorsons Publishers, 1978

Curious Mollusks. Marie M. Jenkins. New York: Holiday House, 1972

Dictionary of Gardening, vol. 4. Royal Horticultural Society. London: Oxford University Press, 1951

Discovering Slugs and Snails. Jennifer Coldrey. East Sussex UK: Wayland, 1987

Easy Gardening. Jack Kramer. Golden CO: Fulcrum Publishing, 1991

Ecological Gardening. Marjorie Harris. Toronto: Random House, 1991

Encyclopedia of Organic Gardening, rev. ed. Emmaus PA: Rodale, 1978

Encyclopedia of the Animal World (Simple Animals). John Stidworthy. Oxford: Equinox Ltd., 1990

Every Man His Own Gardener. Thomas Mawe, 1767

Garden Smarts. Shelley Goldbloom. Chester CT: The Globe Pequot Press, 1991

Gardening for Beginners. Daniel J. Foley. NY: Funk & Wagnalls, 1967

Gardening for Independence. Barbara and Mort Mather. Kennebunkport ME: Durrell Publications, 1978

Gardening Know-How for the '90s. Dick Raymond. Pownal VT: Storey Communications, 1991

General Zoology of the Invertebrates. 4th ed. G. S. Carter. London: Sidgwick and Jackson Ltd., 1961

Growing Food the Natural Way. Ken and Pat Kraft. New York: Doubleday, 1973

Growing Vegetables. Jill Severn. Seattle: Madrona Publishers, 1978

Guide to Invertebrate Animals. 2nd Ed. J. E. Webb et al. London: Macmillan, 1978

Harrowsmith

How Invertebrates Live. Kaye Marsh. London: Phaidon Press, 1975

How to Get Your Lawn & Garden Off Drugs. Carole Rubin. Friends of the Earth, 1989

Huxley's Encyclopedia of Gardening. Anthony Huxley. New York: Universe Books, 1982

Illustrated Encyclopedia of the Animal Kingdom, Vol. 17 (Mollusks). Grolier, 1972

International Wildlife Encyclopedia, Vol. 16. Maurice Burton and Robert Burton, eds. New York: Marshall Cavendish, 1970

Invertebrate Zoology. Robert D. Barnes. Philadelphia PA: Saunders College, 1980

Life of Invertebrates. W.D. Russell-Hunter. NY: Macmillan, 1979

Living Garden. George Ordish. Boston: Houghton Mifflin Co., 1985

Living Things We Love to Hate. Des Kennedy. North Vancouver: Whitecap, 1992

London Observer, June 3, 1990

Miscellany of Garden Wisdom. Bernard Schofield. Philadelphia PA: Running Press, 1990

Moosewood Restaurant Kitchen Garden. David Hirsch. NY: Simon and Schuster, 1992

Mulch Book. Stu Campbell. Pownal VT: Storey Communications, 1991

Natural History of Sex. Adrian Forsyth. Scribners, 1986

New Biology VI, source unknown, from Vancouver Public Library clipping file

New Victory Garden. Bob Thomson. Boston: Little, Brown, 1987

Northwest Gardener's Almanac. Bill Vander Zalm. Surrey BC: Hancock House, 1982

Organic Garden Book. Geoff Hamilton. New York: Crown, 1987

Oriental Vegetables. Joy Larkcom. London: John Murray, 1991

Origins: A Short Etymology Dictionary of Modern English, Eric Partridge. London: Routledge & Kegan Paul Ltd., 1982

Oxford Book of Invertebrates. David Nichols et al. London: Oxford, 1971

Plant Doctor's Rxs for a Healthy Garden. Noel Falk. Harrisburg PA: Stackpole Books, 1991

Practical Gardener. Roger B. Swain. Boston: Little, Brown, 1989

Practical Gardening Encyclopedia. Roy Hay, ed. New York: Van Nostrand Reinhold, 1977

Practical Invertebrate Anatomy, 2nd ed. W. S. Bullough. London: Macmillan, 1962

Q & A: Hundreds of Can-Do Answers to a Gardener's Toughest Questions. Editors of *Organic Gardening* magazine. Emmaus PA: Rodale, 1989

Rodale's Chemical-Free Yard & Garden. Anna Carr et al. Emmaus PA: Rodale, 1991

Rodale's Garden Insect, Disease & Weed Identification Guide. M. Smith and A. Carr. Emmaus PA: Rodale, 1988

Ruth Stout No-Work Garden Book. Ruth Stout and Richard Clemence. Emmaus PA: Rodale, 1971

Seattle Post-Intelligencer

Snails and Slugs. Chris Henwood. London: Franklin Watts, 1988

Sunset New Western Garden Book. David F. Clark, ed. Menlo Park CA: Lane Publishing Co., 1984

Suzanne's Garden Secrets. Suzanne Warner Pierot. New York: Bobbs-Merrill, 1978

Terrestrial Slugs. N. W. Runham and P. J. Hunter.London: Hutchinson & Co. Ltd., 1970

Vancouver Magazine, October 1981

Vancouver Province

Vancouver Sun

Vegetable Growing Handbook, 3rd ed. Walter E. Splittstoesser. New York: Van Nostrand Reinhold, 1990

Vegetables. Judy Newton. North Vancouver: Whitecap, 1991

Weekender's Gardening Manual. Patricia A. Taylor. Toronto: Stoddart, 1986

Western Organic Gardening. Floyd Allen, ed. Emmaus PA: Rodale, 1972

Wise Garden Encyclopedia. Storey Communications. New York: HarperCollins, 1990

Young Specialist Looks at Land and Freshwater Molluscs. Horst Janus. London: Burke, 1965

ACKNOWLEDGEMENTS

Thanks to Min for the waiter pose, Saeko for the Letratone, Peg for the glow-in-the-dark slug, David for the book, Josie for the praise, Steve for the edits and videos. —*E. C.*

Eve Corbel's writings and cartoons appear regularly in *Geist* and *The Mayneliner*, among other publications. She is a Vancouver backyard gardener who has done years of field research on slugs—ever since making the mistake of mulching her entire herb and vegetable garden with hay.

It is the purpose of Little Red Books to gather the essential wisdom of great women and men into single volumes so that students of the Great might judge them in light of their own words, and find where they will the spiritual, sporting and gardening models so earnestly sought after by the young, and so easily forgotten by the old.